Northern Snakeheads Invade Ponds and Watersheds

By Susan H. Gray

21st Century
Junior Library

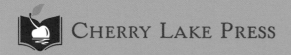

CHERRY LAKE PRESS

Published in the United States of America by Cherry Lake Publishing Group
Ann Arbor, Michigan
www.cherrylakepublishing.com

Reading Adviser: Beth Walker Gambro, MS, Ed., Reading Consultant, Yorkville, IL
Book Designer: Melinda Millward

Photo Credits: © Have Camera Will Travel | North America/Alamy Stock Photo, cover; © jeby69/
iStock.com, 4, 12, 20; © Rainer Lesniewski/Shutterstock.com, 6; © JMP_Traveler/Shutterstock.
com, 8; ©Paulo Oliveira/Alamy Stock Photo, 10, 14; © Bailey-Cooper Photography/Alamy Stock
Photo, 16; © Mosto/Alamy Stock Photo, 18

Cherry Lake Press is an imprint of Cherry Lake Publishing Group.

Library of Congress Cataloging-in-Publication Data

Names: Gray, Susan Heinrichs, author.
Title: Northern snakeheads invade ponds and watersheds / by Susan H. Gray.
Description: Ann Arbor, Michigan : Cherry Lake Publishing, 2021. | Series:
    Invasive species science : tracking and controlling | Includes index. | Audience: Grades 2-3
Identifiers: LCCN 2021004937 (print) | LCCN 2021004938 (ebook) | ISBN 9781534187030
    (hardcover) | ISBN 9781534188433 (paperback) | ISBN 9781534189836 (pdf) |
    ISBN 9781534191235 (ebook)
Subjects: LCSH: Northern snakehead--Control--United States--Juvenile literature. | Introduced
    fishes--United States--Juvenile literature. | Invasive species--Control--United States--Juvenile
    literature.
Classification: LCC QL638.C486 G73 2021 (print) | LCC QL638.C486 (ebook) | DDC 597/.64--dc23
LC record available at https://lccn.loc.gov/2021004937
LC ebook record available at https://lccn.loc.gov/2021004938

Cherry Lake Publishing Group would like to acknowledge the work of the Partnership for 21st
Century Learning, a Network of Battelle for Kids. Please visit http://www.battelleforkids.org/
networks/p21 for more information.

Printed in the United States of America
Corporate Graphics

CONTENTS

Snakeheads get their name from their face shape.

What Is It?

"Look out! It's a snake! No, it's an eel! Oh wait, it's a fish!" A boy was warning people about something on the trail. It was strange, all right. He just wasn't sure what it was.

The animal had shiny scales. Its body was long. There were no legs or feet. The head looked like that of a snake. But it didn't slither along to move forward. It whipped its body back and forth.

Northern snakeheads are native to Russia, China, and Korea.

The boy had spotted a northern snakehead. Since the 1970s, it has been showing up in the United States. People in Maryland, New York, Pennsylvania, and nearby states see the fish often.

The snakehead is an **invasive species** that threatens **native** fish. It can breathe air and live out of water for up to 4 days.

Make a Guess!

People have given the snakehead a nickname. They call it "Frankenfish." Why?

Most snakehead sightings in the United States are in the Northeast.

Frankenfish in America

For years, it was legal to keep snakeheads in the United States. Anyone could buy them at pet stores. **Exotic** food markets offered live snakeheads to buyers.

But sometimes the fish made it into U.S. waterways. Once in a while, a snakehead escaped the food market. Often, pet owners grew tired of their unusual fish. They released their pets into ponds or streams.

Young snakeheads compete with other small fish for food.

In 2002, an **angler** caught a northern snakehead in a Maryland pond. It had grown up to 4 feet (1.2 meters) in length. Fish and wildlife experts were alarmed. They knew the snakehead was an invader. It was a **predator** that could wipe out the native fish. These invaders could easily wreck a pond's natural balance.

Think!

People in Maryland didn't know what kind of fish the angler caught. A fish expert in Florida had to tell them. Why didn't anyone recognize the snakehead?

Snakeheads have no natural enemies in the United States.

Dealing with Invaders

Right away, **fisheries** experts in Maryland got busy. They sprayed a chemical on the snakehead's pond. It killed more than 1,000 young snakeheads. Unfortunately, it also killed other fish. The experts knew the chemical would harm all kinds of fish. But they also knew that the snakeheads had to go. The pond was near a river. If snakeheads got into the river, they could spread rapidly.

Snakeheads live in ponds, lakes, streams, canals, and rivers.
They can also travel on land to another water source.

About this time, government officials looked back to an old law from 1900. That law was written to protect fish and wildlife. It also included a list of **imported** species that could injure other animals. In 2002, northern snakeheads were added to the list. This law can now ban people from buying or selling snakeheads.

Look!

People in Arkansas found the snakehead near the White River. Find the White River on a map and follow its path. What major river does it flow into?

Warning posters tell anglers not to release any snakeheads they catch.

Snakeheads are tough. They can live in water with little oxygen. They are able to withstand cold winters.

Fish experts' best hope is to control their spread. To do this, they are educating the public. Online photographs help people identify the fish. Anglers are told not to release caught snakeheads. Instead, they should kill the fish by freezing it. They should also report the catch to fish and wildlife officers. This helps officers keep track of snakehead populations.

Some places encourage fishing for snakeheads.

Prevention Is Best

Some states have used chemicals to kill snakeheads. But this also kills other fish. Other states have tried killing plant life in the water. This lowers the water's oxygen.

Ask Questions!

Chemicals can kill all the fish in a pond, not just snakeheads. How do pond owners bring back the native fish?

Snakeheads are in more than a dozen states.

Controlling this invasive species will never be easy. The best approach is to keep the fish from taking over new places. This is why experts want to know about every snakehead sighting. They hope to stop new invasions right away.

Controlling an invasive species can cost millions of dollars. It can take thousands of hours. Stopping the entry of an invader is always best.

GLOSSARY

angler (AN-gluhr) a person who fishes with a hook and line

exotic (eg-ZOT-ik) coming from a foreign land; very unusual

fisheries (FIH-shur-eez) places where fish are bred and raised

imported (im-PORT-ihd) brought in from another place

invasive (in-VAY-sihv) not native, but entering by force or by accident and spreading quickly

native (NAY-tihv) occurring naturally in a particular place

predator (PREH-duh-tur) an animal that hunts and eats other animals

species (SPEE-sheez) a particular type or plant or animal

FIND OUT MORE

BOOKS

Ciletti, Barbara. *Northern Snakeheads*. Mankato, MN: Black Rabbit Books, 2017.

Kalman, Bobbie. *Invasive Animal Species*. St. Catharines, ON, Canada: Crabtree Publishing Co., 2016.

Metz, Lorijo. *What Can We Do about Invasive Species?* New York, NY: PowerKids Press, 2009.

WEBSITES

Academic Kids—Northern Snakehead
http://www.academickids.com/encyclopedia/index.php/Northern_Snakehead
Learn about some of the problems snakeheads are causing.

AquaKids—Snakeheads
https://www.youtube.com/watch?v=foUx8n9Msdk
Watch this 21-minute video to see how people are dealing with this invasive species.

Chesapeake Bay Program—Northern Snakeheads
https://www.chesapeakebay.net/S=0/fieldguide/critter/northern_snakehead
Find snakehead basic information and fun facts here.

INDEX

ABOUT THE AUTHOR

Susan H. Gray has a master's degree in zoology. She has written more than 180 reference books for children and especially loves writing about animals. Susan lives in Cabot, Arkansas, with her husband, Michael, and many pets.